Program Authors

Diane August
Donald R. Bear
Janice A. Dole
Jana Echevarria
Douglas Fisher
David Francis
Vicki Gibson
Jan Hasbrouck
Margaret Kilgo
Jay McTighe
Scott G. Paris
Timothy Shanahan
Josefina V. Tinajero

Cover and Title pages: Nathan Love

www.mheonline.com/readingwonders

Send all inquiries to:
McGraw-Hill Education
2 Penn Plaza
New York, NY 10121

ISBN: 978-0-07-679559-8
MHID: 0-07-679559-4

Printed in the United States of America.

2 3 4 5 6 7 8 9 RMN 20 19 18 17 16 A

Start Smart **Let's Get Started**

The Big Idea: What do we need to learn?

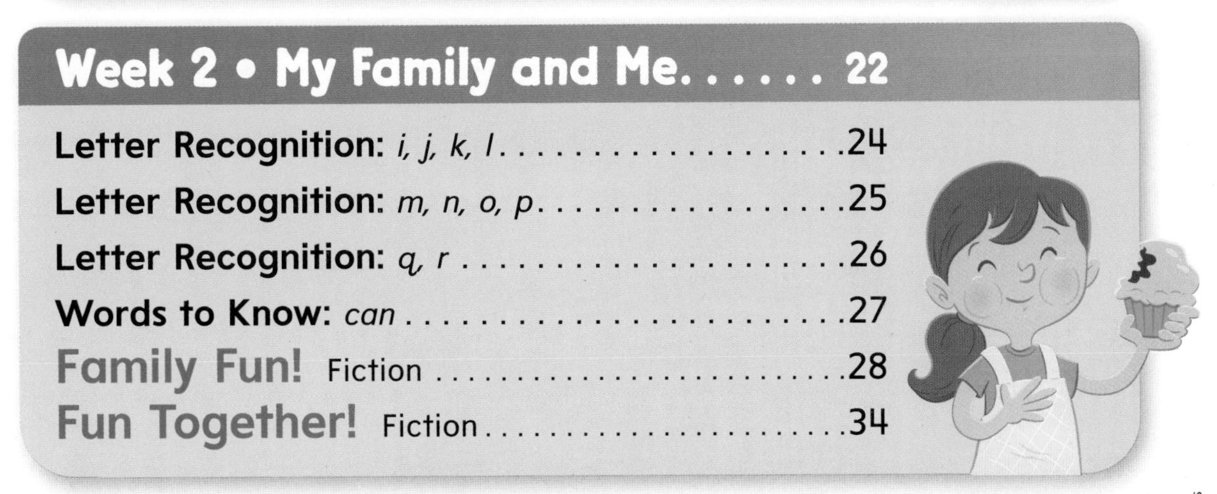

Essential Question

How is everyone special?

Go Digital!

Talk About It

How are these children special?

Ariel Skelley/Blend Images

Look At Us!

Aa

Bb

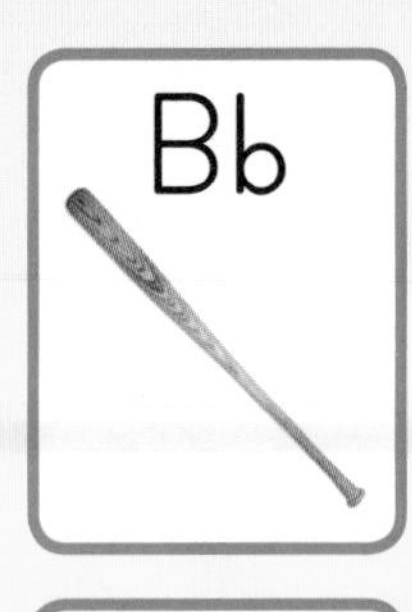

Cc

Dd

Ee

Ff

Gg

Hh

Ii

Jj

Kk

Ll

Mm

Nn

Oo

Pp

Qq

Rr

Ss

Tt

Uu

Vv

Ww

Xx

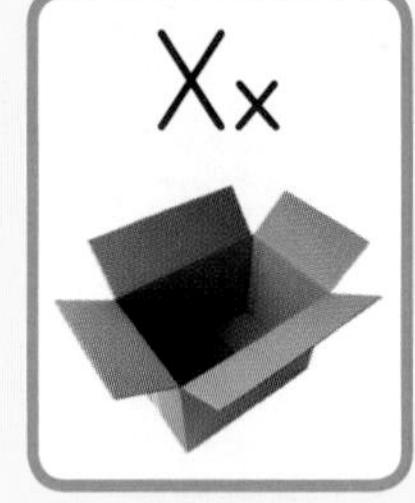

Yy

Zz

(alphabetically) Stockdisc/PunchStock; Radlund & Associates/Artville/Getty Images; Photodisc/Getty Images; imagebroker/Alamy; Pixtal/AGE Fotostock; Comstock Images/Alamy; Jules Frazier/Photodisc/Getty Images; Royalty-Free/Corbis; Photodisc/Getty Images; RubberBall Productions/Getty Images; Royalty-Free/Corbis; C Squared Studios/Photodisc/Getty Images; Photodisc/SuperStock; Photographers Choice RF/SuperStock ; Photo Spin/Getty Images; Joshua Ets-Hokin/Photodisc/Getty Images; Steve Cole/Photodisc/Getty Images; 97/E+/Getty Images; Ingram Publishing/Fotosearch; Stockbyte/Punchstock/Getty Images; Westend61/Getty Images; Photodisc/Getty Images; C Squared Studios/Photodisc/Getty Images; D. Hurst/Alamy; Image State/Alamy

Say the name of each letter.

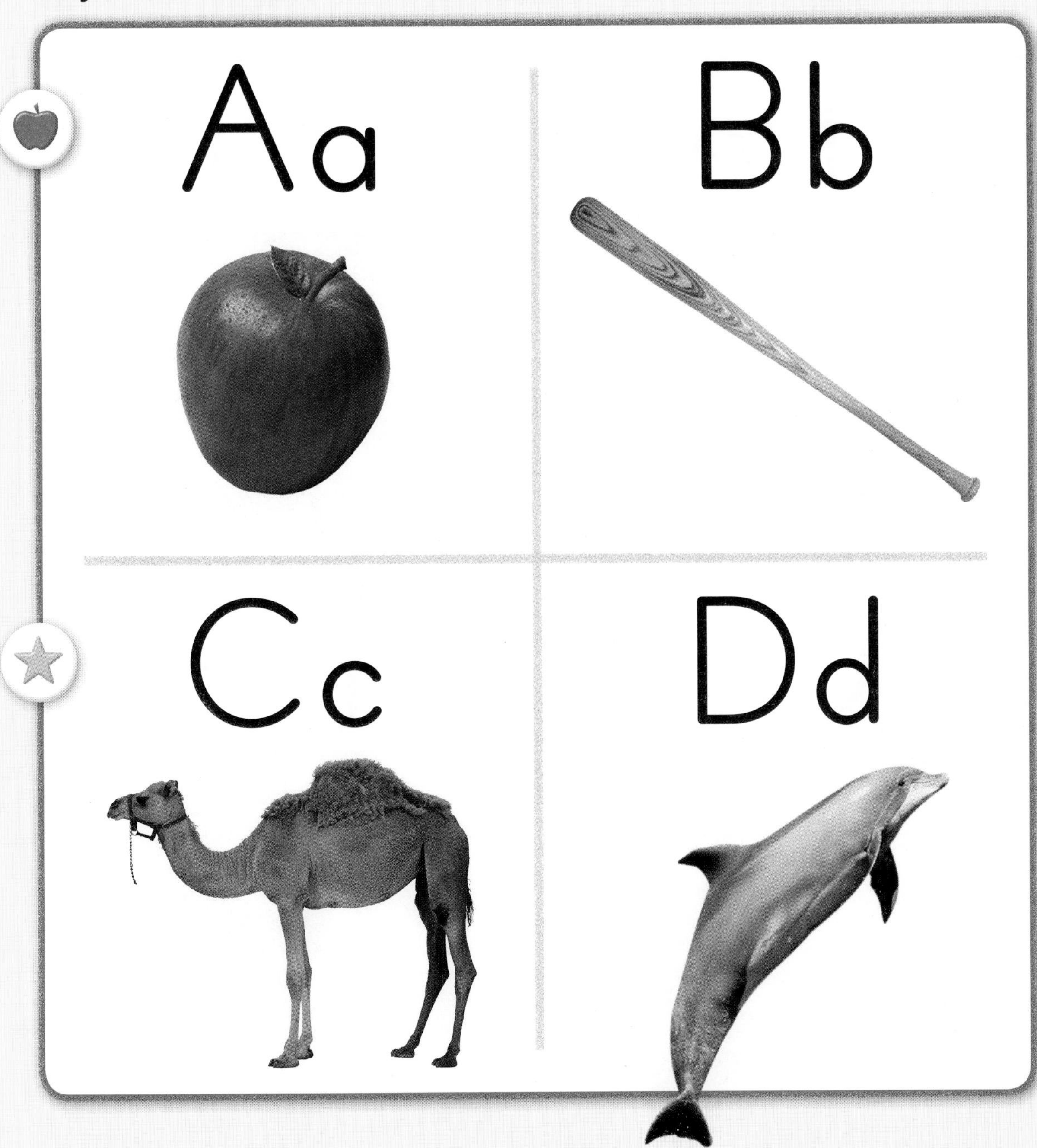

Letter Recognition

Say the name of each letter.

(tl) Pixtal/AGE Fotostock; (tr) Comstock Images/Alamy; (bl) Jules Frazier/Photodisc/Getty Images; (br) Royalty-Free Corbis

Words to Know

Read Together

I

I can play.

I can skate.

(t) Fabio Cardoso/Corbis; (b) Dennis MacDonald/age fotostock

I Am Special!

Molly Idle

Molly Idle

Molly Idle

Molly Idle

Molly Idle

The End!

Molly Idle

Look at Me!

Liza McCorkle/Vetta/Getty Images

I  .

jump

(t) Brian Kennedy/Flickr/Getty Images; (b) Caroline Hu

I  .
dance

I  .

paint

(t) Jose Luis Palaez, Inc/Blend Images/Corbis; (b) Caroline Hu

I  .

read

(t) Picture Partners/Alamy; (b) Caroline Hu

I  .
write

(t) Sharie Kennedy/LWA/Corbis; (b) Caroline Hu

Weekly Theme My Family and Me

Essential Question
Who is in your family?

Go Digital!

Jack Hollingsworth/Photodisc/Getty Images

Family Times

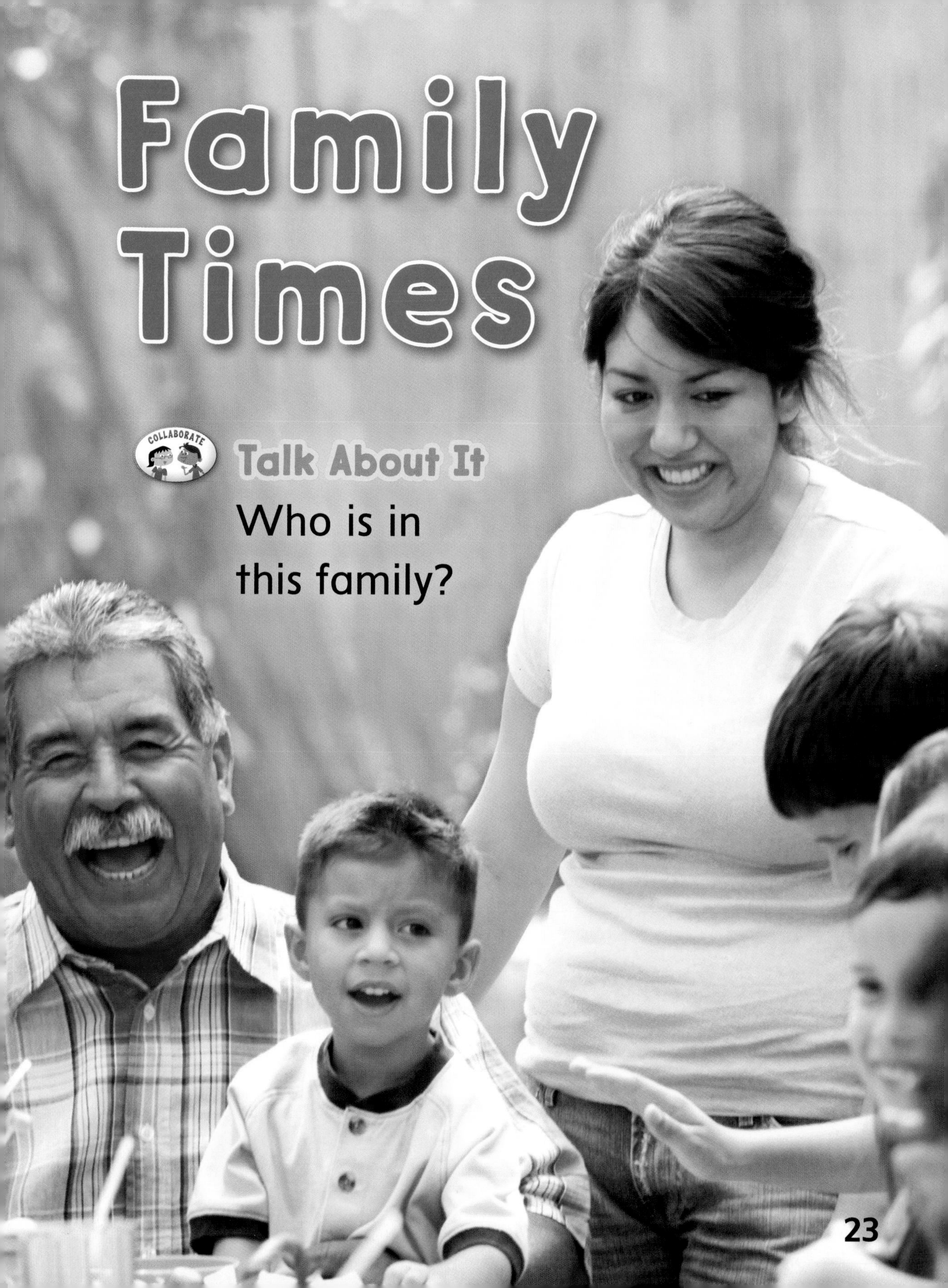

Talk About It

Who is in this family?

Say the name of each letter.

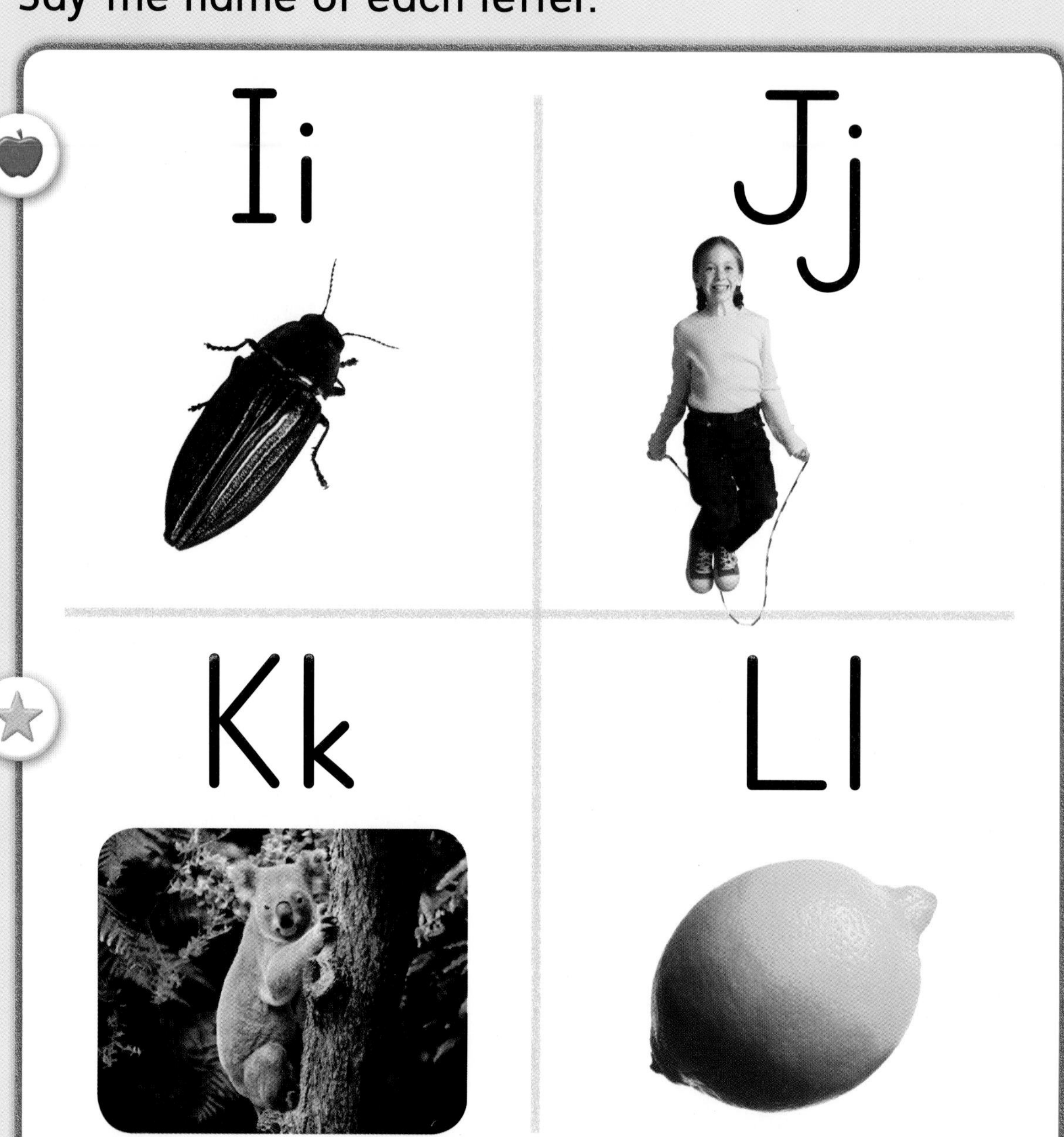

Say the name of each letter.

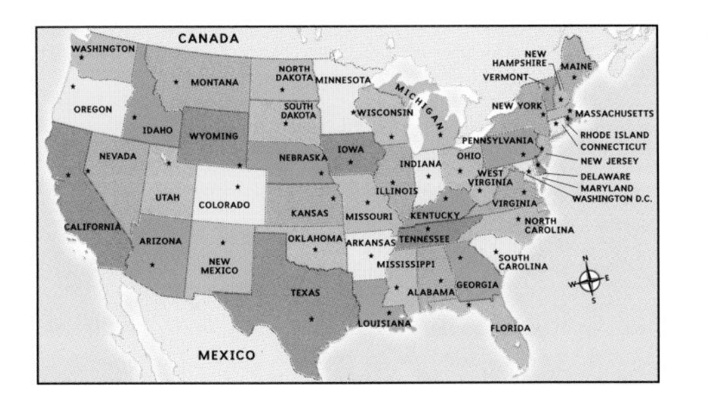

O o

P p

(tl) McGraw-Hill Companies, Inc.; (tr) Photodisc/SuperStock; (bl) Photographers Choice RF/SuperStock; (br) Photo Spin/Getty Images

Say the name of each letter.

Qq

Rr

(t) Joshua Ets-Hokin/Photodisc/Getty Images; (b) Steve Cole/Photodisc/Getty Images

Words to Know

Read Together

can

Tim **can** ride.

Can I go?

(t) Stunning images/Alamy; (b) GK Hart/Vikki Hart/Stone/Getty Images

Family Fun!

Valeria Cis

Valeria Cis

Valeria Cis

Valeria Cis

Valeria Cis

Valeria Cis

Fun Together!

Katie McDee

I can pour.

Katie McDee

I can  .
mix

Katie McDee

I can bake.

Katie McDee

I can clean.

I can  !

eat

Katie McDee

I Can Do It!

Talk About It

What can this girl do?

Jose Luis Pelaez/Iconica/Getty Images

Letter Recognition

Say the name of each letter.

(tl) 97/E+/Getty Images; (tr) Ingram Publishing/Fotosearch; (bl) Stockbyte/Punchstock/Getty Images; (br) Westend61/Getty Images

Say the name of each letter.

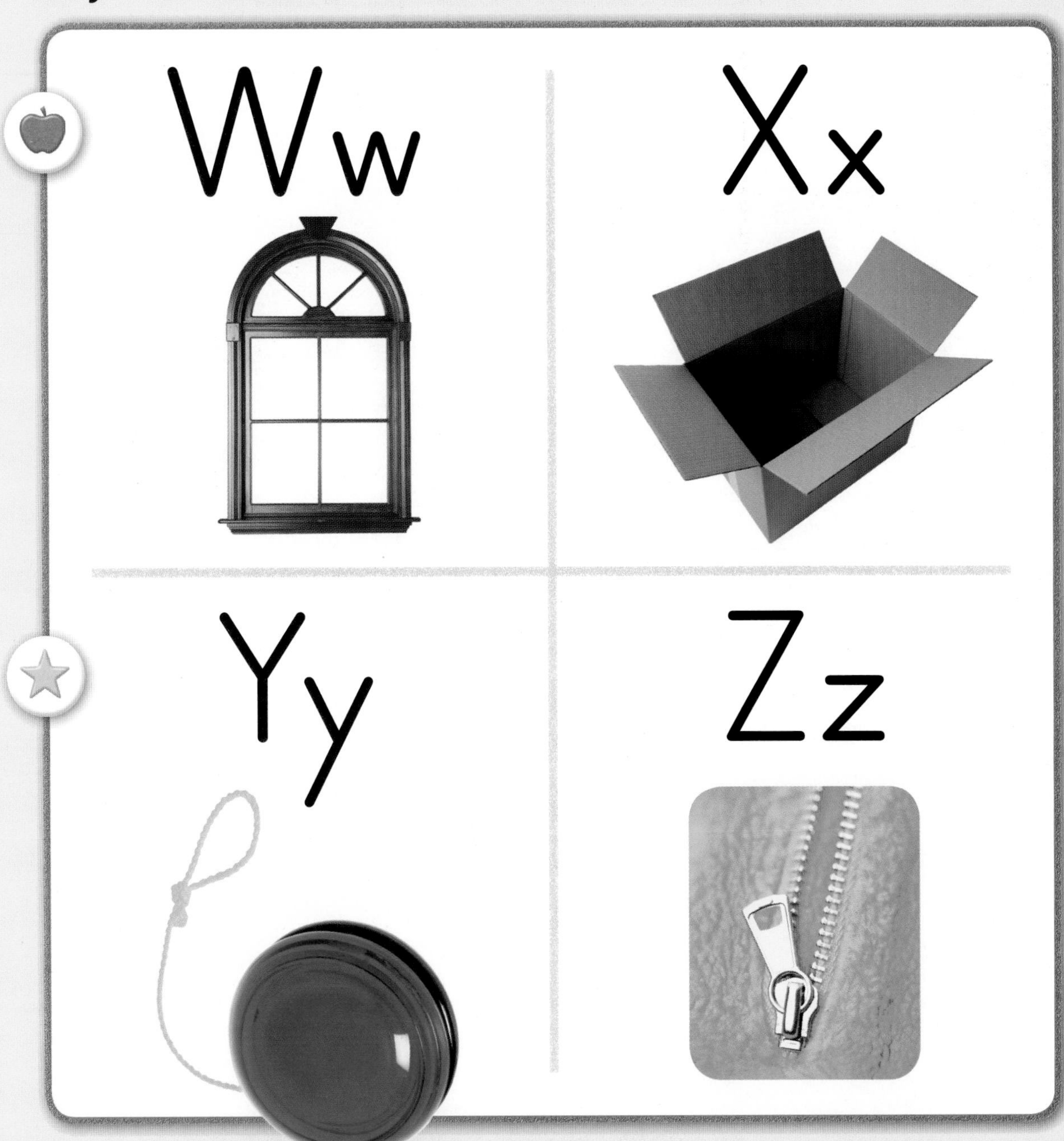

Words to Know

Read Together

I **can**

I **can** help!

Can **I** play with Ana?

At School

Robin Boyer

Robin Boyer

Robin Boyer

Robin Boyer

Robin Boyer

Robin Boyer

What Can I Do?

Tom Stewart/Corbis Bridge/Alamy

I can .
ride

(t) Andrew Kornylak/Aurora Photos/Alamy; (b) Caroline Hu

I can  .

rake

(t) LWA/Dann Tardif/Blend Images/Getty Images; (b) Caroline Hu

I can .

walk

(t) Stella Luna Photography/Flickr/Getty Images; (b) Caroline Hu

Can I  ?

read

(t) Henglein and Steets/Cultura/age fotostock; (b) Caroline Hu

(t) Joey Celis/Flickr/Getty Images; (b) Caroline Hu

I can  !
read